31-Day Devotional for Lupus Warriors

Dr. De'Andrea Matthews

Scripture quotations are from the ESV® Bible (The Holy Bible, English Standard Version®), copyright © 2001 by Crossway, a publishing ministry of Good News Publishers. Used by permission. All rights reserved.

Edited by:
Shairon L. Parks
SLT Inspirations LLC

Published by:
Claire Aldin Publications
P.O. Box 453
Southfield, MI 48037

Library of Congress Control Number: 2019948094
ISBN: 978-1-7336560-6-1
Printed in the United States of America.

FOREWORD

As a lupus survivor, two things that helped me to persevere has been my faith in God and knowing that God is a healer. In April 2006, I founded Sisters Acquiring Financial Empowerment (SAFE), a nonprofit organization designed to help survivors of domestic violence overcome the economic effects of abuse. Later that year, an autoimmune disorder took the life of one of my aunts and a few weeks later, I was diagnosed with lupus.

I knew that God had many things He wanted me to accomplish, so why would this happen to me? Through prayer and obedience, God showed me that He wanted me to continue despite any diagnosis. The most important part was to have faith and maintain my doctor's appointments. Despite any circumstances, I must trust and believe in God.

Oftentimes, lupus survivors or warriors are dealing with multiple physical challenges in addition to other burdens of life. A daily practice of intentionally putting God first will help you to be victorious over lupus and any other challenge in your life.

De'Andrea Matthews is a multi-dimensional woman of God—wife, mother, pastor, author of many books, book publisher who has had lupus directly affect her family. She is passionate about guiding lupus warriors to maintain and increase their faith.

I was very excited when I heard that she was creating this devotional. I know that this devotional will bless all who read and dedicate themselves to this phenomenal 31-day journey of faith.

The "31-Day Devotional for Lupus Warriors" is more than a book; it is a valuable tool that will increase your faith, hope and trust in God. I highly recommend this book for you and as a gift for someone you know who has been challenged with lupus.

~Kalyn Risker Fahie, Founder
Sisters Acquiring Financial Empowerment (SAFE)

A NOTE FROM THE AUTHOR

When someone joins the armed forces, they often leave behind what is familiar and learn to depend on strangers to defend the cause while protecting each other's lives. This is how I view our relationship. You don't know me, and I don't know you; but we are united for the same cause.

31-Day Devotional for Lupus Warriors was birthed as I sat in intensive care with my daughter, Tiara Wiggins, unable to assist in any substantive way with her recovery. Only six months into her diagnosis, the physician told her she was at risk for sudden cardiac death. After traveling over 1200 miles to be by her side, I wondered how I could be of greater help to her and others.

You see, I was introduced to lupus about 30 years ago when my older sister, Leoler Shanklin, was diagnosed. Just shy of adulthood at the time, I felt the same void—not knowing what could be done or how. As if that wasn't enough, two weeks into launching the ministry God gave me in spring 2018, we lost a dear member and friend, Angela Scott, to lupus. Later that same year, my niece, Ar'Lynda Matthews, was diagnosed with lupus nephritis. The disease was impacting more and more people in my immediate sphere of influence. The foundation had been laid and it was time to act.

As president and founder of Claire Aldin Publications and senior pastor of Visions International Ministry, I chose to use the best of who I am to empower those who identify as and provide care to lupus warriors. Whether you are fighting the disease or supporting a loved one with the disease, this devotional is for you.

I presented the idea of creating a devotional to my daughter, Tiara. While she was yet undergoing numerous tests and procedures, she created the cover image for this devotional. You can see more of her artistic talent by following her @twiggscreative on Instagram.

Ten percent of the proceeds from the sale of this devotional will be donated to Lupus Detroit. The remaining proceeds go directly to support the medical expenses of my oldest daughter and lupus warrior, Tiara Wiggins, who will soon "age off" my health insurance. We are endeared to you for your support.

~Dr. De'Andrea Matthews
President and Founder, Claire Aldin Publications

TABLE OF CONTENTS

Day 1
You Make Me Stronger

The king is not saved by his great army; a warrior is not delivered by his great strength.

~Psalms 33:16

Just like in this passage of Scripture, we, as warriors, cannot depend on our physical, mental or emotional strength to get us through each day. We must depend on Someone higher than us—the One who is all-knowing, mighty, and powerful.

In what ways have you tried to do it on your own? Make a decision today to ask God to show you how to depend more on Him to make it through each day.

Day 2
Roller Coaster

But Moses' hands grew weary, so they took a stone and put it under him, and he sat on it, while Aaron and Hur held up his hands, one on one side, and the other on the other side. So his hands were steady until the going down of the sun.

~Exodus 17:12

Life was never meant to be lived in isolation. While in the midst of battle, even the leader of God's people needed support. His "support staff" kept him steady when he grew tired from the battle waging on. Moses could only win when his hands were up, so Aaron and Hur were a part of that winning team.

Some days, you will feel up. Others you will feel down, just like a roller coaster. Who is your support in this battle? Write down the names of at least two people who you can call on when you grow tired and weary.

Day 3
Kick Start

So we do not lose heart. Though our outer self is wasting away, our inner self is being renewed day by day.

~2 Corinthians 4:16

Your physical body may go through many changes, but today's devotion reminds you not to lose heart. Regardless what the body looks like on the outside, as you grow closer to God, your inner being grows stronger day by day. After all, you are a spirit in a body with a soul.

Jot down an affirmation to remind yourself who you are in Christ. Let this reminder kick start your day!

Day 4
Oxygen Mask

The Spirit of God has made me, and the breath of the Almighty gives me life.

~Job 33:4

Some days, you may not feel like being here. It gets hard to breathe knowing all that is yet ahead to fight for and/or against. In a clinical setting, you would need an oxygen mask when it becomes difficult to breathe.

This Scripture is a reminder that God is the One who gave you life. He chose you for a purpose. That purpose may not be clear right now, but you are still a treasure in the eyes of the Almighty. Choose at least one way to give thanks today.

Day 5
Boxing Ring

The Lord will fight for you, and you have only to be silent.

~Exodus 14:14

Perhaps today is one of fatigue. Physically, you have nothing left to give. It is in those times that you need to know that the Lord will fight for you; just be silent before Him.

You are not in this battle alone. Those standing around the boxing ring waiting to see the outcome are cheering for you. Today, think of one success that you can celebrate. Let that be your victory chant. You can win!

Day 6

Metamorphosis

Jesus Christ is the same yesterday and today and forever.

~Hebrews 13:8

As your body goes through changes, it may feel like a total metamorphosis. Know that our Lord Jesus Christ remains constant and loves you. When you feel like everything around you is changing, hold onto Jesus who remains loving, giving and true.

Today, write about a time that you learned of Jesus' love for you. In what ways has He shown His love directly or through other people?

Day 7
The Gift

For the wages of sin is death, but the free gift of God is eternal life in Christ Jesus our Lord.

~Romans 6:23

It is at different phases of life that people accept Jesus Christ as their Lord and Savior. Even if you have relatives who are "saved," you still must accept Him as your own. Have you accepted the gift of salvation that Jesus offers? If not, repeat these words:

Dear Lord, I acknowledge that I need you. I believe you died for my sins to reconnect me to my Heavenly Father. I confess with my mouth and believe in my heart that you are my Lord and Savior. As I receive you, You receive me, in Jesus' name. Amen!

Day 8

Finding Your Way

And she said, "Let your servant find favor in your eyes." Then the woman went her way and ate, and her face was no longer sad.

~1 Samuel 1:18

Hannah, the woman described in this Scripture, believed God for a miracle when it looked like all hope was lost. The priest, Eli, joined her in prayer asking that her petition be granted. Her faith, combined with another's, lifted her spirits and helped her find her way back to a place of peace which showed on her face. You know what else? She got the miracle she prayed for.

What are you praying for? Have you shared your petition with someone who can stand with you in prayer?

Day 9
Road Signs

So that those who dwell at the ends of the earth are in awe at your signs. You make the going out of the morning and the evening to shout for joy.

~Psalms 65:8

Nature speaks to the awesomeness and beauty of our Creator. The next time you are traveling and stop at a road sign, look for evidence of the wonders of God. They are in the sky, in the trees, and all around. Take a moment to embrace His presence.

What do you like the most in nature? Take a photo or capture that symbol in art. Art is good medicine!

Day 10
Heart of the Matter

The precepts of the Lord are right, rejoicing the heart; the commandment of the Lord is pure, enlightening the eyes;

~Psalms 19:8

A percept is a mental impression gained through the five senses. Through the Lord Jesus, our spiritual senses can be activated as well. Dreamers receive from the Lord through their eyes in dreams while they are asleep. They receive visions while they are awake. He wants you to "see" what lies ahead, to enlighten your view and give you something to rejoice about.

What good news are you anticipating? Can you find the promise in His Word that confirms it is yours? This is something to rejoice about!

Day 11
Holiday Buffet

Oh, taste and see that the Lord is good! Blessed is the man who takes refuge in him!

~Psalms 34:8

Psalms 34 is a song of thanksgiving. King David is praising God for delivering him from fear and from trouble.

Have you ever been feeling a little afraid then realized the holidays were coming up? Thinking of all that good food, including some of your favorites being prepared, made those other thoughts disappear. We see the food first, then we taste it, which confirms its goodness.

It's the same way with God's Word. We see it when we read it. We taste it when we experience God's best for us. When His promises manifest in our lives, that's something to be thankful about.

When was the last time you gave thanks? What are you thankful for? Write down five things that you are thankful for, and place the note where you can see it daily to remind you to give thanks in all things (1 Thessalonians 5:18).

Day 12

Footprint

Your way was through the sea, your path through the great waters; yet your footprints were unseen.

~*Psalms 77:19*

It is easy to start thinking that God is not with you in times of despair, particularly when we have been trained to believe the tangible objects we see every day. Just because His footprints can't always be discerned doesn't mean He is not there.

Just as the Scripture above states that His footprints were unseen, the evidence of His presence is still with you. Identify evidence of God's existence and His care for you in your surroundings. Remember, He often uses other people to demonstrate His love as well.

Day 13

Seeds

It is like a grain of mustard seed, which, when sown on the ground, is the smallest of all the seeds on earth,

~Mark 4:31

In its context, this Scripture is referring to the kingdom of God, a vast support network of believers in Jesus Christ. Similarly, a seed has no value without its connections. In order to grow, the seed must be placed in the ground. That setting requires not only a relationship with the soil around it, but also with the sun and the water. This relationship will provide nourishment for it to be sustained and accomplish its purpose in the earth.

When it seems darkest, remember that you are a seed among many. Don't negate your relationships. Reach out to those connections for nourishment and to sustain you when you need it most.

Day 14
Declaration

O Lord, open my lips, and my mouth will declare your praise.
~*Psalms 51:15*

There may be days when you don't feel like opening your mouth. You won't feel like talking to anyone. You may not even want to talk to yourself. You are entitled to those moments — you are going through so much! But, as a good friend once told me, you only have 24 to 48 hours to be in *that* space. Loving you means helping you to continue this journey in spite of not feeling like it.

These twelve words can make a huge difference. Even if it's all you say, repeat these words. When you cannot do it on your own, the Lord will be your strength. Put a praise on your lips!

Day 15

Agreement

Again I say to you, if two of you agree on earth about anything they ask, it will be done for them by my Father in heaven.

~Matthew 18:19

When was the last time you came into agreement with someone? No, I'm not talking about something that is legally binding. What about something fun? A lot of times, when this Scripture is used, it's to talk about agreement in prayer. It's great to have someone agree with you on your prayer requests—I hope you have done that, as well. But this time, I want to focus on something to which you can look forward.

Today, select a friend to hold you accountable. Agree with them on doing something fun that you miss. Give yourself a timeline so you will have some wiggle room. Whether it's watching the sunset, blowing bubbles, visiting the Grand Canyon or simply taking a walk on the beach, do something for you that you really enjoy. Cross a trip off your bucket list and don't forget to smile as the day approaches. You deserve it!

Day 16
Flowers

The flowers appear on the earth, the time of singing has come, and the voice of the turtledove is heard in our land.

~*The Song of Solomon 2:12*

Flowers often appear after the rain. Rain can represent many things in your life. Whatever the rain represents, the flowers will bloom. Look for their beauty all around you.

Do you have a favorite flower? Have you shared what it is with anyone? Let someone know what your favorite flower is, then focus on what you like best about it. Even if you're allergic to flowers and cannot enjoy their actual presence, a still photograph is just as beautiful to behold.

Day 17

Fruit

But the fruit of the Spirit is love, joy, peace, patience, kindness, goodness, faithfulness, gentleness, self-control; against such things there is no law.

~*Galatians 5:22-23*

The word "is" is singular, yet there are nine characteristics listed. Should it then say, "The fruit of the Spirit are..."? Have you ever considered that love is the singular fruit that we are called to have and the other eight are demonstrations of love? If the fruit of the Spirit is love, then joy, peace, patience, kindness, goodness, faithfulness, gentleness, and self-control are all expressions of the love God has towards us.

Think about an orange. It is a single fruit; yet, when you look inside, there are different pieces of that orange which can be shared. Find one small way to express love to another. You'll be surprised how one text message, handwritten note, or phone call can mean so much.

Day 18
Tokens

Show me a sign of your favor, that those who hate me may see and be put to shame because you, Lord, have helped me and comforted me.

~Psalms 86:17

Do you remember going to an arcade or game room and receiving the small tokens as a reward? Those tokens could then be taken to the counter and redeemed for a prize. On the token is usually printed that it cannot be redeemed for cash. The value to the recipient is not in monetary value.

You may have heard the expression, "a token of affection." The token represents the exchange for something small compared to the value it represents, yet a powerful reminder that you're winning. What small token reminds you that you're winning? Whatever that token is, look at it as a reminder that there is a winner in you.

Day 19

Love Letters

Grace to you and peace from God our Father and the Lord Jesus Christ.

~2 Thessalonians 1:2

Above is just one of the opening greetings from the letters that Paul wrote to the church at Thessalonica, which is in modern day Greece. He often wrote letters to the churches that he started, encouraging the pastor and the congregation to endure in spite of their circumstances. With love letters, it isn't always to the person with whom you are romantically involved. Some love letters are to let the other person know that you're thinking of them and you care.

Have you ever received a love letter? Have you ever written a love letter? Writing seems to be a lost art in the age of technology, but it does the heart good. Today, sit down and write someone you love a letter. If you're feeling up to it, mail it to them. If not, keep it, reflect on it or start your own journal of letters about things you love.

Day 20
Power Surge

Be angry and do not sin; do not let the sun go down on your anger,

~*Ephesians 4:26*

A power surge can mean different things to different people depending primarily on your age. In this instance, a power surge refers to getting hot all of a sudden. I don't know about you, but when it gets hot, I can get irritated. When I'm irritated, it's a lot easier to get angry over little things. The goal is not to let those little things spiral into big things.

The Bible teaches us not to let the sun go down on our anger. When does the sun go down near you? Most often, it's between 6 p.m. and 7 p.m. I always thought I had until midnight to get rid of my anger before the new day came in. Read that again. Don't let the sun go down...It's not worth it to let that anger fester. People are important, so let's work to maintain the relationships we have and not let anger rule the day.

Day 21
Fresh Wind

And let us consider how to stir up one another to love and good works, not neglecting to meet together, as is the habit of some, but encouraging one another, and all the more as you see the Day drawing near.

~Hebrews 10:24-25

Congratulations on making it to Day 21! Research shows that if you can maintain a task for 21 days, it becomes a new habit. You now have a new habit of encouraging yourself.

Today's Scripture reminds us to encourage one another, so think of someone you can encourage. Just like you need encouragement, someone else does, too. Sharing encouragement is like fresh wind on a summer afternoon. Spread the love!

Day 22
Dawn of a New Day

And the Lord answered me: "Write the vision; make it plain on tablets, so he may run who reads it.

~Habakkuk 2:2

Each new season of our lives brings direction and purpose. We are not on this earth to just work and pay bills. It's the dawn of a new day. You can go forth with renewed purpose and vision for what is to come.

What do you feel God is calling you to do in this season of your life? What dream are you thinking about? What vision has God shown you? Take a moment to write it down and give a few action steps to move in the direction of your destiny. Today is a good day to start again.

Day 23
Travels

Every place that the sole of your foot will tread upon I have given to you, just as I promised to Moses.

~Joshua 1:3

In this life, we never know where our travels will take us. The road that you have traveled to get to where you are today is unique to you. Your background, your experiences are all a part of your journey, and there is still more to add.

The wisdom that you've gained can help shape someone else's journey. Reflect on how a quote or Scripture helped you, then take a moment to share one pearl of wisdom from your own journey on social media to help someone else.

Day 24

Rest

And on the seventh day God finished his work that he had done, and he rested on the seventh day from all his work that he had done.

~*Genesis 2:2*

Are you a workaholic? Are you constantly trying to get a number of things done at one time? Does it seem like there is a never-ending to-do list with your name on it? If this describes you, know that there will always be expenses and there will always be tasks to complete; but even God rested.

Celebrate the small successes and remember to get the rest that your body needs. We need you rested and refreshed.

Day 25

Family Reunion

Then Joseph could not control himself before all those who stood by him. He cried, "Make everyone go out from me." So no one stayed with him when Joseph made himself known to his brothers.

~Genesis 45:1

Things happen in life that sometimes cause us to separate from our family members. Time does not heal wounds; only the Holy Spirit can heal wounds. As believers in Jesus Christ, it is up to you to be open to receiving healing whenever and however the Lord sends it to you. Regardless of whose fault the separation was, God is all about restoration. He wants to restore family.

Think of one person that you miss, never met, or would like to reconnect with. Pray about it then decide what you can do to bridge the gap just as Joseph did with his brothers.

Day 26
Redeemed

You have led in your steadfast love the people whom you have redeemed; you have guided them by your strength to your holy abode.

~Exodus 15:13

Who doesn't love coupons and discounts? You're able to get the item that you want without spending the full price. Well, redeeming a coupon is only vaguely similar to being redeemed by God. God paid full price through the redemption of the blood of Christ for the remission of our sins. What does that mean? Regardless of who has discounted you in this life, even when we discount ourselves, God knows your true value.

When you start to feel down and wonder if any of this is worth it, know that your worth is not in the tangible things around you, but the value that your Creator placed in you from eternity. You are valuable and loved by the Almighty God who sacrificed it all just for you.

Day 27
Pinky Promise

And the Lord will make you the head and not the tail, and you shall only go up and not down, if you obey the commandments of the Lord your God, which I command you today, being careful to do them,

~Deuteronomy 28:13

Have you ever made a "pinky promise"? A promise is a promise, but did that one seem more real? Sometimes as children, we will make a pinky promise to do something, not understanding the full weight of what is being asked or given. That's not the case here. God has made over 8000 promises in His word to His people. He is more than capable of keeping every promise.

In today's Scripture, it is a reminder that God wants us as the head and not the tail. He wants His people in leadership, not just following blindly behind someone else. Continue to obey the word of the Lord and trust every promise in His word.

Day 28
Courtesy Cup

Remind them to be submissive to rulers and authorities, to be obedient, to be ready for every good work, to speak evil of no one, to avoid quarreling, to be gentle, and to show perfect courtesy toward all people.

~*Titus 3:1-2*

Restaurants used to be very open to providing courtesy cups of water to its patrons. A courtesy cup meant that you didn't have to pay extra to get some water—a necessity in this life. Unfortunately, some restaurants now want you to purchase a bottle of water or pay for the cup instead of providing it for free. Even though society is changing about how it is courteous to others, the people of God are called to show perfect courtesy toward all people.

Being kind, or showing courtesy can be a lost art, so meditate on how you can be mindful not to speak evil. Endeavor to be gentler in your interactions. It can make a difference to the person you least expect.

Day 29

Bruised Fruit

The earth brought forth vegetation, plants yielding seed according to their own kinds, and trees bearing fruit in which is their seed, each according to its kind. And God saw that it was good.

~Genesis 1:12

Growing up as a little girl, there were fruit trees in our backyard. We had apples and pears galore. My grandmother would have us pick up the fruit that had fallen to the ground. I hated that job because I had to fight the bees off. Although the fruit may have gotten bruised in the fall, the bees found something valuable to their existence in the fruit. My grandmother took the fruit we collected and made the most delicious homemade jelly and pies. You see, she didn't care that the apples and pears were bruised; she would just cut the bruised part off and use the rest in her recipes. I learned that you don't throw the whole thing away just because it's bruised.

We get bruised in relationships, at work, and in life. Today, think of how you can cut away the impact of your bruises so you can flourish and provide sustenance to those around you.

Day 30
Healing

But he was pierced for our transgressions; he was crushed for our iniquities; upon him was the chastisement that brought us peace, and with his wounds we are healed.

~Isaiah 53:5

When you want to get something different, you must do something different. We have been conditioned to grumble and complain so much that it seems normal. As those who were made in the image and likeness of God, our words have power. What we speak has the power to manifest, so we need to learn to declare what God has already decreed. He said that with Jesus' wounds, we are healed. It's already done, even when it has not manifested in the earth realm or in your doctor's reports.

Today, begin to declare that you are healed. Believe it and receive it in Jesus' name.

Day 31

Press Reset

For if you forgive others their trespasses, your heavenly Father will also forgive you,

~Matthew 6:14

Are you willing to do everything possible so you walk in freedom? If so, it starts with understanding that forgiveness does not mean that what the other person did was right. Forgiveness allows you to release the pain to the Creator so He can handle it. Forgiveness is like pressing reset. You get the blank canvas to begin again.

Choose forgiveness. Pray that God brings healing to your heart and release it to Him. He cares for you more than you realize. Choose freedom. Let go and let God.

ABOUT THE AUTHOR

Dr. De'Andrea Matthews is an author, award-winning publisher, international speaker and the senior pastor of *Visions International Ministry*. As the mother and sister of two lupus warriors, this devotional is a personal tribute to them while encouraging other lupus warriors on their journey. Inspired to pave the way for many to grow spiritually and professionally, many lives will unquestionably be positively impacted by and through Dr. De'Andrea Matthews.

Special discounts are available on bulk quantity purchases by support groups, book clubs, associations or other special interest groups. For details, email **info@clairealdin.com** or call (248) 571-8227.

Claire Aldin Publications is an award-winning, hybrid publisher. A proud member of the Independent Book Publishers Association (IBPA) with Better Business Bureau Accreditation, our mission is to diversify publishing by producing nonfiction titles for authors from diverse backgrounds.

Want to know more?
Write to us at info@clairealdin.com
or call 248-571-8227

www.clairealdin.com

Connect with us on social media:

@clairealdin